LIFE IN INDIA

Owing to the antiquity and rarity of this book, certain pages are regrettably absent, and readability is compromised due to the blurring of the original text. If you possess any insights regarding the availability of these missing sections, kindly inform us. Your assistance is crucial in ensuring the completion of this significant work for the benefit of future generations.

LIFE IN INDIA.

BY

MAJOR THE HON. C. DUTTON

GYAN

Published by

Gyan Publishing House
5, Ansari Road
Daryaganj, New Delhi-110002
Phone: 011-47034999, 9811692060
E-mail: books@gyanbooks.com

Distribution Network
gyanbooks.com
India, USA, Canada, UK, Australia

ISBN: 978-93-6280-037-4 (PB)
First Published, 1882

2nd Impression 2024

Printed at: Gyan Press, Delhi.

LIFE IN INDIA
Author: MAJOR C. DUTTON

LIFE IN INDIA.

LIFE IN INDIA.

BY

MAJOR THE HON. C. DUTTON.

LONDON:
W. H. ALLEN & CO., 13 WATERLOO PLACE,
PALL MALL. S.W.

1882.

LIFE IN INDIA.

CONSIDERING what an important part of the British Empire India is, and how many of the British not only visit it but depend on it for a livelihood, it is wonderful how little is known in England about the country, and how unprepared those going out generally are for what they may find there.

The two principal classes of Europeans in India are the soldiers, who really hold the country, and the members of the civil service, who attend to the collection of revenue, administration of justice, and the general working of the laws. Besides these, there are the mercantile classes which are mostly to be found in the presidency towns of Calcutta, Madras, and Bombay, and the planters, who cultivate indigo, tea, coffee, &c., and I think there is no doubt that this latter class is increasing yearly.

Life in India has changed very much within the last forty or fifty years, chiefly owing to the greater ease and rapidity with which visits can now be made to Europe. In former days, men who joined the Indian army or civil service did so knowing that India would be their home for the greater part of their lives, and that until they finally quitted the country their visits to Europe would be few and far between. They consequently laid themselves out for life in their new homes, spent their money there, and dispensed the hospitality for which India has always been famous. But there is a great change in this respect now-a-days. The facilities for getting to Europe are much greater, and short periods of furlough are more easily obtainable than they were formerly; consequently the chief thought with European officers is to live carefully in India, and save up all their pay to be spent on visits to England. Officers frequently go home now on three months' leave, which, deducting the time spent on the passage home and out again, gives about six weeks in England. Supposing such visits are made every three years, with now and then longer ones, extending to one or perhaps two years, it is obvious that when they are provided for, much money will not remain to be spent in India.

There is another thing which has constituted a serious loss of late years to Europeans living in India, and that is the loss in remitting money to England. The rupee is supposed to be worth two shillings, and in size and make is very much like a florin. Till about thirteen years ago, this could be remitted to England at the equivalent of two shillings, or very nearly that, but for some time past, owing to depreciation in the value of silver, the rupee has not been worth quite one shilling and eight pence, and the consequence is that a person wishing to send, say one hundred pounds to England, has to pay rather over twelve hundred rupees, or 20 per cent. to do so. Considering how many Indian officials there are who have children to be brought up in England and other expenses there, it can be easily understood that this loss by exchange is a very serious matter; for salaries have not increased in India—rather the reverse, if anything—while expenses, as in all countries with which the English have to do, have very decidedly increased—almost doubled within the last fifty years, some people say.

That branch of the army which belongs to the Queen's service, as it is called in contradistinction to the Indian service, mostly travels backwards and forwards between Great Britain and India in H.M.'s Indian troopships, than which it would be hard to find a finer mode of conveyance; in fact, I believe these troopships are the finest of their sort in the world. Officers of the Queen's service coming to England on leave on private affairs, officers of the Indian military service, and officers of the Indian Civil Service, have to provide themselves with passages, and usually employ the ships of the Peninsular and Oriental Company. These also are very fine ships, and if speed is an object, the plan is to go by Venice or Brindisi, and thence across the Isthmus of Suez by the Canal. By this route, Bombay can be reached from London in nineteen or twenty days. Some people though, who have families or who wish to avoid all the changes inseparable from using this route, or who may be good sailors and not averse to a sea voyage, prefer taking ship at Gravesend, and they will then be about twenty-eight days in getting to Bombay.

The P. and O. ships, as they are usually called for the sake of brevity, travel at a higher rate of speed than the troopships, but they stop at Gibraltar, Malta, Port Said, Suez, and Aden, while the troopships, as a rule, stop only at Malta and Port Said. There are other ships running between England and India also which convey a considerable number of passengers, and they ply from London, Southampton, and Liverpool to Bombay, Madras, and Calcutta; but the P. and O. certainly carries the largest number of passengers; firstly, because it is the oldest established company, possessing a large fleet of very fine ships, and it has been for years noted for having very efficient officers and crews; and, secondly, because, as the Company has a contract with Government for the carriage of the mails, the journey has to be performed within a certain time, and passengers feel sure of being landed at Bombay by the date on which they have calculated. Personally, I have only been to and from India in one of H.M.'s troopships, so I know nothing of the quicker route across Europe and by Brindisi. The first place we stopped at was Malta, and I must say I should not care to remain there any length of time. There is plenty to interest and amuse one for a few days, but there must be a great sameness about life in Malta, and the people who get on best there are those who are fond of yachting, for which it does very well.

The old Roman Catholic churches in the chief town, Valetta, are most interesting, with their pictures and monuments, and there are beautiful orange gardens in the interior of the island which are well worth a visit. In Valetta there is a very fine Opera House, where there is a good opera every winter, which can be attended for prices that seem very moderate when compared with London ones; and there is an excellent club for those who reside in the island, and to which visitors can obtain access if they have friends who are members of it. In fact, when you leave Malta you part company with European life, and your next experiences will be of the East.

The next place at which the ship stops is Port Said, a small town at the Mediterranean mouth of the Suez Canal, and here coal is taken in. There is nothing of any interest to be seen here. The place has only sprung up since the opening of the canal, and though it has increased very much lately, and will probably increase still more, the only thing to take one ashore is to make purchases of fruit or other things one may happen to want, or to inquire for letters which are sometimes sent to the post-office there to await arrival. Coaling over, the ship proceeds through the canal, and while doing so, it is impossible to help feeling that one sees a very wonderful piece of engineering. Ships propel themselves through the canal, going at a slow rate, and time has shown that the banks wear far better even than the promoters of the scheme anticipated. There is, of course, a considerable amount of traffic through it, and ships continually pass each other, one lying in a bay cut out of the bank while the other passes. About the middle there are some natural lakes called the "Bitter Lakes," and ships often anchor in one of these for the night, as they all have to spend a night somewhere in getting through the canal.

There is nothing of any interest or beauty

to be seen in passing it, little but sandy desert on either side; but it is a great comfort to avoid the change from ship to train and then back again to ship, which had to be made before the canal was opened, especially as in doing so one had to make the acquaintance of fresh officers, and commence everything *de novo*.

Suez, which is at the other end of the canal, is uninteresting too, but it is soon left behind and one is steaming away down the Red Sea, the most noticeable feature of which is its excessive heat, which is present for the greater part of the year. Some people do, and some do not, know what clothing they should take with them for wear on the voyage; and though it depends very much on the season of the year, still it is necessary to have clothes of different thickness for different parts of the voyage, no matter when the journey is made. For securing a favourable temperature throughout, the best time to go is in the very depth of winter; for if you go by Brindisi, you soon get from the cold of England to the warmth of the Mediterranean, and the heat from Suez to Bombay will never be disagreeable. Should you go at this time by Gibraltar and Malta, the journey will be very cold till the Mediterranean is entered, and up to that point it will be necessary to have plenty of warm clothes which can be gradually laid aside till Suez is reached, when a complete change of costume will be necessary. Perhaps the hottest portion of the whole journey is the Red Sea, and there are only four months in the whole year, viz. January, February, November, and December, when this can be called at all cool. It is hot, but very bearable, in June, July, and August, while the monsoon is blowing, but at other times of the year it is suffocating.

Travellers who have nothing to do with India, but who simply go out there during the winter to see the country or get sport, generally leave England about the end of September or beginning of October, and start on their homeward journey again towards the end of March, that is to say before the hot weather sets in. These are the men who never can understand what Englishmen have to complain of in India, and think they are very much overpaid. They forget the years that are spent in exile away from home and away from friends, and they know nothing of the days that are spent shut up in a house, with the thermometer ranging from 90° to about 105°, or of the nights when the unhappy Englishman tosses about with not even a sheet over him, and totally unable to sleep for the heat. Indian officers, too, very often go to England at the commencement of the hot season and return when the cold is setting in, for by this means, if they take eighteen months furlough, they secure two summers in England which is a great object, as the winters in India are enjoyable enough.

No matter when you go, though, you should have changes from under-clothing upwards ready for wear at Suez, and the best plan is to have these packed in a separate portmanteau and lodged in the baggage-room to be got up while passing through the canal.

There is no doubt that a journey to India presents fine opportunities to anyone who wants leisure for reading and writing, for it is not an easy matter to get through the long days on board ship. Most people naturally take books with them, but on H.M.'s troop-ships, and, I believe, on the P. and O. ships as well, there are very good libraries, which, if not filled with the newest books, at any rate contain a good many one has never read, and a good many of histories, travels, and biographies, which are always interesting, no matter when they are read.

There is one way in which some of the travellers to India pass away the time on board ship, and a very useful way it is too, and that is by learning something of the Hindustani language. It is, I suppose, one of the most easy in the world to learn, both as regards grammar and pronunciation, and, armed with Dr. Forbes's *Hindustani Manual* and his dictionary, it is wonderful how much colloquial knowledge you may attain in the month passed between Gravesend and Bombay.

Besides its heat, the other point most noticeable about the Red Sea is the intricacy of its navigation, at any rate as compared with the other portions of the voyage, and more wrecks occur in it than anywhere else on the whole journey. The Southern Cross here first becomes visible, but seen so far north it is a very poor constellation, and rather disappointing to those who expect to find in it a rival to the Great Bear and other of the northern constellations. To be viewed at its best it should be seen much further south, south of the Cape of Good Hope in fact, but it is never so distinct and marked as the Great Bear. At the entrance to the Red Sea from the Indian Ocean is the Island of Perim, which is held by a detachment of native infantry, relieved every three months from Aden. A more dreary abode for the British officer in command of the detachment it is hardly possible to conceive, as he is the only European on the island, and consequently entirely without society.

There is an old story told in India on this subject to the following effect, but I should be very sorry to vouch for its accuracy. Formerly the detachments at Perim were only relieved every six months, and some years ago a subaltern was stationed on the island who, when the time for his relief was approaching, applied for permission to remain with the new detachment. The general who had to sanction the arrangement was somewhat astonished at the application, but thinking that the officer was perhaps of a studious turn of mind and anxious for an opportunity of reading without disturbance, or possibly wished to remain there for financial reasons, consented without demur. He was still more astonished when at the end of the year the same officer applied for permission to remain on in the island, but still he raised no objections to the arrangement. In the meantime the General went to England on leave, and one morning when walking down Pall Mall, the first person he met was the subaltern whom he had supposed to be safe in the island of Perim! The secret was out, and the General no longer wondered at his young friend's apparent love of solitude.

After leaving the Red Sea, it does not take long to reach Aden, and though troopships do not often stop there, the P. and O. steamers always do. It is a dreary place and by no means popular as a station; a fact of which the Government of India show their appreciation by relieving the British infantry regiment there every year.

Aden suffers from a very scanty water-supply, and about three or four miles inland, situated amongst low rocky hills, are some large and curiously constructed reservoirs which serve to catch whatever rainfall there is, and on which the cantonments are principally dependent for their water. These are really the only things at Aden worth seeing, and most people, I fancy, are glad when the ship steams away, whether it be towards England or India. In the latter case land is not again sighted until Bombay is reached, and here commences the traveller's first experience of Indian life.

He will soon find himself besieged by servants wanting employment, and these will be of different races. Of course if he is remaining in the Bombay Presidency, there will be swarms willing to take service with him, as this is their home; if he is going to Madras, he may find a few Madrassees anxious to return to their own country, or some Bombay men may be willing to go with him; but if he is going to the Bengal Presidency, he will find a considerable number of servants who have come down to Bombay with masters who are leaving India, and especially if they have not had their return fares paid they are anxious to get service with someone who will give them free passage up country again. I have heard it said that such servants should never be employed, but I cannot say that I see any reason for this. You may, of course, pick up a bad one, but so you may anywhere; while on the other hand, if a master takes but one servant down to Bombay to wait on him until he goes on board ship, it is only likely that he would take the best he has, and if there be any truth in this, the person arriving in Bombay from England ought to have a choice of rather good servants than otherwise. At any rate I have known several cases of servants engaged at Bombay remaining with their masters for years after; and even if they do not suit, there is no difficulty in changing them, for this is much more easily managed in India than in England.

Legally, I believe, servants out there can claim a fortnight's warning, but practically this is never given; and if a servant does not answer, it is much better both for him and his master that he should be changed as soon as possible. If it did not suit the servants they would very soon apply to the magistrates, for they rarely hesitate to take out summonses against employers by whom they consider themselves ill-treated.

In India the system is not as in England, to write to a servant's former employer and ask for a character of him, but on dismissal each servant, if fit to have a character at all, receives one written on a sheet of paper—a *chit*, as it is called in the language of the country. In this matter I fear there is a feeling, which obtains also in England very much, of smoothing away defects, and saying as little as possible to a servant's disadvantage. Even when a servant has been a very bad one you will too often find the master saying, "Oh, poor wretch, I won't say anything to prevent his getting another place," and so makes the most of any virtues he may have had, but carefully avoids saying anything of his failings. As soon as the *chit* is given, the recipient goes off to someone in the bazaar who can read English, and asks him what his master has said. If the character is not as favourable as he wishes, back he goes and commences whining about the damage his late master is doing by giving him so bad a one. "Is he (the master) not his father and mother? Does he wish to starve his children?" &c.; and he goes on in this way till the master, worried out of all patience, very likely tears up the character, and gives another not penned so strictly according to truth as the first, but more in accordance with the wishes of the recipient.

A servant at all advanced in years will probably produce a considerable bundle of these characters, and they may all be genuine and the property of a very good servant, or not. In the first place they are considered of so much value that they are frequently stolen and sold for (what are to people in that class of life) considerable sums of money. Then they are bequeathed by one relation to another, and they are occasionally lent for a consideration, until the borrower is suited with a situation; and in all of these cases the name given in the characters has to be assumed by the person using them, so though masters employing servants always ask them their names, they very rarely have the wrong ones given them.

It is a good plan when engaging a servant, unless he has been handed over to you by a friend who knows all about him, to keep these characters, enclosing them all in an envelope inscribed with the owner's name, and putting them away, at any rate for some time, till you see what sort of a bargain you have got. If the owner objects to your keeping his characters, you may be pretty certain that they do not belong to him, and you had better have nothing to do with him; but if he is willing to leave them in your hands it is easy to keep them for a time, and if the man turns out well and you do not want to be troubled with his characters, you can always return them to him.

Most people would be inclined to engage, at any rate, one servant at Bombay, and especially if going up country with troops, as in this case several days would be spent on the journey, and the best man to get would be one who would do valet and wait at table also. I might as well say here that no one must expect to find an Indian servant like a really good English valet. They have no idea of packing whatever, and simply cram clothes and other articles into portmanteaux anyhow. Then they know nothing of cleaning boots, breeches, &c., as an English servant would do, and altogether are not to be compared to the latter. It is absolutely necessary to have them though, for, supposing people could afford the expense of European servants, they are not suited to the country, and this is clearly shown by the fact that even officers in the army give up their soldier servants, and when they do keep them on, only employ them to clean swords, gloves, guns, &c.

Ayahs who perform the duties of nurses or of ladies' maids are, if anything, still more inferior. Not one in five hundred knows anything about doing hair; and as for dressmaking or even mending, of this they are equally ignorant. However, they are useful in different ways, and if a lady landing at Bombay has any children with her she will find it almost essential to get an ayah before starting on her journey "up country." There is no doubt that Madras ayahs are very much the best in India, and though they require better wages than Bengali ones, they are, if good, well worth the money. For one thing, they speak English really well and fluently, which is a great convenience to a lady arriving in India for the first time, and they are much more like English servants in all their ways than the ordinary ayahs are; the only thing is that like Madras men-servants they are very difficult to get good out of their own country. However, whatever native servants she may employ, I would recommend every English lady who has children, and can at all afford it, to take out an English nurse with her. Hitherto, it has occasionally been possible to obtain fairly good nurses from amongst the soldiers' wives in India, but it is never possible to reckon on their staying for any length of time, and, moreover, it must be remembered that, under the new army organisation, there will not be many married people to choose from.

Having said so much on this subject, I would devote a few words to Bombay before carrying my readers away to the interior. In my opinion this is the finest of all the presidency towns; for though Calcutta is the head-quarters of the Government of India, and is called the City of Palaces, I never could see much of the palace description about it, with the exception of Government House, which undoubtedly is a very fine building. Otherwise, Bombay has far finer buildings than anything I ever saw in Calcutta, and it has, besides, the advantage of being most beautifully situated on the sea, while Calcutta is built on the banks of the Hooghly, which is anything but a pure river, and some miles from the Bay of Bengal. Running out from Bombay into the sea, is a sort of spur called Malabar Hill, which affords a very fine situation for houses, with which it is covered, the Governor amongst others having one there.

There are several different hotels in Bombay, the largest being Watson's, which is somewhat on the principle of the Langham and other large London hotels. I have heard all of these establishments more or less abused, but I will leave any of my readers, who may ever visit India, to form their opinions for themselves. The shops in Bombay are good enough, in fact better than anything that will be found in the country except in Calcutta or Madras, for the smaller stations can compete in this respect with the presidency towns even less than country towns in England can compete with London.

One great requirement of Bombay at present is a new cathedral, for in this respect it is not nearly so well off as Calcutta or Madras, and, in fact, has to put up with a very ordinary church, not nearly so good as those to be seen in many stations in India, which is dignified with the name of The Cathedral. The service is very well conducted there though, and in the matter of singing it is ahead of any other church I ever was in in India.

There is one thing which everyone before leaving Bombay must furnish himself with, and that is bedding; for it is one of the peculiarities of the country, that wherever you travel you take your bedding with you. Bed-linen you will probably have brought out from England, and possibly blankets also, but the remainder you will have to get in Bombay. Wherever you go you will find in your room a bedstead, or, in the language of the country, *charpoy*, which is simply a wooden frame covered with cotton webbing, and very comfortable bedsteads they are. In most bazaars, and certainly in a large town like Bombay, there is no difficulty in getting *resais*, which are quilts made of some bright-coloured and generally rather flashy-patterned chintz, thickly lined with cotton wool. Some people in India use mattresses, but *resais* are more convenient when travelling, and it is the custom to spread out one of these to lie upon; possibly, if the weather is cold enough, using another as a covering over the top sheet, unless blankets are used, which I think preferable. However, having bought one or two of these *resais* and a pillow, the traveller is fitted out with his bedding, if he possesses linen, and he will then only require a waterproof sheet, and a couple of straps to roll it up with when it is not spread out. It is just as well to take all such things out from England, ready for use, as they cost double the price if bought in India.

The principal reason for this taking bedding about is that it is so frequently wanted in railway journeys or journeys by road, which often extend over several nights, and this was much more the case in former days than now. When travelling by train in India, either first or second class, every person is entitled to as much space as will enable him to lie down at full length, and with this view the carriages are made on an entirely different pattern to those in England. Every European traveller going first or second class, and those of the higher ranks amongst the natives, have their bedding with them, and when evening approaches make regular preparations for turning in.

In former days, very long journeys had to be made by *dooly dâk*, the meaning of the former word being the conveyance in which the passenger travelled, a sort of oblong box or framework, with curtains, long enough to lie down in, suspended by iron rings from a long pole. This was carried by four men at a time, six or eight men accompanying the dooly at once and being relieved every four or five miles, with spare men for the luggage, whence the word *dâk*, which means stage or staging. This mode of conveyance is still in use over some roads in India, though it has been a good deal superseded by carriage dâks. In the beginning of the century, journeys in India took an enormous time; for even in going up country, people had to go the whole way by dooly dâk, and you cannot reckon on more than four miles an hour by this mode of conveyance.

A story is told of Bishop Wilson (who was Bishop of Calcutta, and who in this respect really seems to have been the Bishop Wilberforce of India, for all sorts of stories are told about him), that once a young chaplain just out from England was staying at the Palace in Calcutta, and after being there for some little time had at last quite made up his mind that he was to remain and be one of the cathedral chaplains. The first intimation he had that this was not the case was one morning at family prayers, when the Bishop said, "And we beseech Thy especial protection for our young friend, who is about to undertake the long and arduous journey to Peshawar." As this meant a journey of over twelve hundred miles to be mostly performed by dooly dâk, the young chaplain's surprise was not agreeable.

Travelling by carriage dâk was as great an improvement on the dooly as the railway is on the carriage; but though not so expensive as the dooly, still it was and is a costly mode of locomotion. The carriages are heavily built, something on the pattern of a four-wheel cab, only longer, and in using them the traveller can either lie down at full length or sit up, as he pleases. If he wishes to do the latter, he puts his feet into a well there is in the centre of the carriage; but if the former, the well, which can be filled with small parcels, such as travelling-bags, &c., is covered over with a padded top, and the bedding is then spread out at full length in the carriage, and this is the way travellers almost always use them—when night comes, if the weather is cold, closing the doors, which do not open and shut by hinges, as in ordinary carriages, but slide backwards and forwards. Unless the passenger pays for the whole carriage, he may find another person put in with him, which will naturally make a very great difference in his comfort; but this does not often happen, except at times or over roads where there is a great pressure of business. On the roof of the carriage the luggage is piled, and there is sufficient room for one or two servants to sit with their chins resting on their knees, in which position they sleep as peacefully as if they were lying on the most comfortable beds.

The lithesomeness of an Oriental is something wonderful, and comes from the limbs being accustomed to be doubled up in all sorts of positions from the earliest childhood. That sort of double-jointedness which English acrobats only acquire by constant practise from the time they are three or four years old, comes quite naturally to every Oriental.

The carriages are drawn by two ponies; one in a pair of shafts, and the other hooked on alongside him, and these are changed almost every five miles. Some of the dâks are managed by Government, and these, though the most expensive, are much the best, and as a rule travel at a considerable pace; I have known them in some cases average nine and ten miles an hour including stoppages. Those which are managed by private companies are not nearly so well horsed, but even with the best there is frequently a difficulty about getting the animals to start. Many of them are bought because they are so vicious their owners can do nothing with them, and no doubt they find a considerable difference in their new life, when they get regular, not to say hard work, and by no means an over-abundance of food. You very soon find out the sort of animals you have to do with. The harness, which is of the simplest pattern, being arranged, the coachman mounts the box; then commence shouting, tugging, swearing in Hindustani, pushing at the wheels, and every method which can be employed to induce a start. Sometimes the animals go off in the meekest manner, at others it takes some minutes to get the vehicle in motion, during which it seems very doubtful whether the whole turn-out will not be smashed to pieces; but I must say that once started, the ponies generally go as hard as they can tear till the next post is reached, when the same ordeal probably has to be gone through with the fresh pair.

Accidents are not altogether unfrequent, for the carriages are but roughly made by local builders, and consequently wheels come off, etc., or possibly the ponies upset you in a ditch, but it is wonderful how little actual damage is done, and in all the years I spent in India I hardly ever heard of anyone being the worse for one of these accidents.

Before proceeding further I would say that I only served in the Bengal Presidency, and know but very little of Bombay, and nothing at all of Madras, except by hearsay; but Bengal, by which I mean the country under the Lieutenant-Governors of Bengal, the North-Western Provinces, and the Punjâb, and more directly under the control of the Viceroy, is the principal portion of India; and besides, though there may be some minor differences, the mode of life all over the country is very much the same, being governed by very similar conditions and climate. The different presidencies have their advantages in different ways; for instance, I think Bengal would admit that in the way of plains' stations it has nothing to compare with Poona, in Bombay, or Bangalore, in Madras. These are really magnificent stations, and though situated on the plains and not in the hills, and having railways running to them, they are considerably elevated above the sea, and consequently free from the extreme and oppressive heat which makes ordinary stations in the plains so trying. Poona, too, is no very great distance from the sea, and thus gets the benefit of the sea air, which is such a want in the greater part of the country.

Having said this, let us suppose ourselves travelling towards Upper India, which from Bombay as far as Jubbulpore will be over the Great Indian Peninsular Railway, and after that over the East Indian Railway. Of late years a new system of spelling Indian names and words, invented by Dr. Hunter, has come into use, and by this, Jubbulpore would be spelt Jabalpur, and Meerut, for example, Mirat, but I have thought it best to adhere to the old-fashioned way, for in most cases the words look as they ought to sound; Jubbulpore, for instance, can only be pronounced as it ought to be, the only change that could be made to render the proper pronunciation more certain would be, perhaps, to spell it Jubblepore; whereas if I adopted the Hunterian method, most people would inevitably pronounce the words wrong.

Soon after leaving Bombay the line commences ascending some hills or *ghâts*, as they are called here, and for a time there is a very curious specimen of railway travelling. The line has to make considerable ascents and goes zig-zagging about in a very peculiar way, in fact you will at times find yourself going in exactly the opposite direction to that in which you were going a few minutes previously. This portion of the journey has to be done very slowly, and with engines made specially for the purpose; but the scenery in these ghâts is extremely pretty, and the time (if by day) does not seem long before the top is reached, and the train once more speeding onwards in the usual manner.

The ordinary traveller will have got into a carriage at Bombay which runs right through, without changing, to Allahabad, and will be about thirty-six hours on the road. I should have mentioned that Indian first and second-class railway carriages are all fitted with washing apparatus, so there is no more difficulty in dressing than there is in going to bed in them. The train stops long enough at certain stations to enable the traveller to get his meals, and it struck me that the refreshment-rooms between

Bombay and Jubbulpore were better than any others I had met with in India.

An officer going up country with troops would be longer on the road, as there are rest barracks at certain intervals, where the troops are disembarked from the trains and kept for twelve hours or so. It is not, of course, possible to provide every soldier, woman, and child with lying-down accommodation in a train, and consequently it is necessary to make frequent halts for rest, and to enable them to get the meals which are provided for them at these rest barracks or camps as the case may be.

I would here make some remarks about railway travelling as it is usually conducted in India, for it differs in many respects from that in England. Although railways are largely used by the natives, the companies do not seem to find that it pays them to run many passenger trains in the day, and the usual number over the different lines are one in the morning and another in the evening. There may be one, or at the most two, more running in the course of the day, but these are generally between stations not far apart, and are intended to meet purely local requirements. At the same time the goods traffic must pay well, for it has usually been the case in India, before starting a railway company, for the Government to guarantee a dividend of five per cent., and I believe I am correct in saying that in most cases this rate and even more has been earned by the companies for themselves very soon after the opening of their lines.

Accidents occur very rarely, and, indeed, there would be little excuse if it were otherwise, as the speed is very moderate, and the only thing which ever seems to increase it is the time wasted at railway stations while the guards are talking to their friends or otherwise dawdling about, which necessitates the train being pushed along somewhat to make up the loss. Of course the risk of accidents is very much diminished by there being so few trains run, and another thing which tends in the same direction is the fact that almost all the lines are only single gauge; the one exception to this rule being, I believe, a comparatively short bit of about two hundred miles from Calcutta up the East Indian Railway. I must confess, though, my wonder that there have never been any accidents at any of the marvellous railway bridges in the country, and I can only say that the absence of them is a striking testimony to the ability of the constructors, and points to these bridges as perfect specimens of engineering skill. Any-one who has passed over the bridges across the Ganges at Cawnpore and Rajghât, and over those across the Jhelum and Sutlej, which vary in length from two miles downwards, must admit that the railway engineers in India have well carried out the work entrusted to them.

Almost all the plains' stations in Upper India east of Lahore can now be reached by train, or at least those which are military stations can be. There are some few, such as Seetapore and Ferozepore, which are military stations, and smaller ones where only civilians reside, which still lie off the lines; but the railway system has been so developed of late years that they cannot any of them be at a very great distance from it. In October, 1880, the Punjab Northern State Railway, running from Jhelum to Rawal Pindi, was opened; and when this is completed to Peshawar, which it very soon will be, there will be an unbroken line of railway from Calcutta to Peshawar.

Where the stations do not touch the railway, they almost invariably have excellent roads running to them, with dâk carriages plying at very reasonable rates. When talking about dâk travelling, I might have mentioned that there are, I suppose, few countries in the world which have finer roads than India. In the first place they are mostly very level, and they are, as a rule, kept in very good order. They are divided into several classes. The first class are metalled and bridged throughout. The second class are fairly good roads—bridged, but not metalled everywhere; and though perhaps dog-carts could be used over them, they would not do for dâk carriages. After these, if I remember aright, there are two more classes, the last being simply country lanes, and, as regards wheeled conveyances, only fit for bullock-carts.

The metalling is done with a substance called *kunkur*, which looks somewhat like petrified clay, very hard, and suitable for road-making, which is dug out of pits in small pieces. When a road requires mending it is picked up where necessary, *kunkur* laid down on the picked parts, and after it has been well saturated with water it is beaten into the road with iron rammers by gangs of coolies.

All the roads along which dâk carriages ply are metalled, and it would be hard to find a finer one than the Grand Trunk Road, which runs from Calcutta to Peshawar, a distance of over twelve hundred miles, and which was, until recently, a first-class road, metalled throughout. A first-class road I suppose it still is, but the growth of the railway system has made this road of somewhat less importance than it was formerly, and I believe a few small portions of it here and there are no longer metalled, but it is still of immense value, and will ever remain a monument of British engineering in India.

Places in the country where the English have settled down are always called stations, and partly, I suppose, from the difficulty of finding any other name by which to describe them. Towns or villages would not be applicable, because the houses are built too far apart, though these names are used and are correct enough in describing native communities. In stations, houses are built more or less separately from one another, and usually each is surrounded with a good-sized piece of grass land called its "compound."

There is a very great difference in stations in

India, chiefly owing to difference in size, and consequently in importance, and it is not by any means the largest which are always the most pleasant to live in, though in almost all there is no lack of society. Every station of any importance has its club, and people meet at each others' houses daily, to play whatever game happens to be in vogue. Formerly it was croquet; then that was superseded by badminton; now nothing is thought of but lawn tennis, and a capital game for India it is too, bringing people together, and inducing them to take exercise when otherwise they would probably feel too languid to move out of their chairs. It is on account of this that we so seldom see retired Anglo-Indians settled down in the country in England. They have for the greater part of their lives been accustomed to meet their friends at one house or another almost daily, and English country life is to them insupportably dull. Consequently, when they have finally done with India, they settle in London, Cheltenham,

Bath, Edinburgh, Dublin, or somewhere where they can be sure of finding or making friends, and seeing them constantly.

Having brought our traveller up the line as far as Allahabad, it will, perhaps, be as well to say something about that place before going further. It is a very large station, measuring several miles each way, and for some years past it has been growing in importance. One cause of this is that it is the capital and the winter residence of the Lieutenant-Governor of the North-Western Provinces,* and the High Court or head-quarters of the law courts of the North-Western Provinces are here also. Then it is a very important centre of railway traffic, as the East Indian Railway passes through it and has its branch

* There is no particular reason that these should now be called the North-Western Provinces, except for the difficulty of finding a fresh name. Previously to the annexation of the Punjab, they did constitute the extreme north-west boundary of the British possessions, but now they lie somewhere in the centre of British territory in upper India.

line running towards Bombay from it; besides, there is here a large establishment of railway workshops, all of which increases the European population of the place. It is, too, the head-quarters of a division of the Bengal army, and though it has not so many troops quartered in it as some stations have, this is rather fortunate, as it is by no means very healthy, and is not unfrequently visited by outbreaks of cholera. In India, summer and winter are always spoken of as the "hot weather" and the "cold weather," and in Allahabad the hot weather sets in somewhat early—in fact, I think punkahs are in use there in March, and they are kept at work till well into November. On the other hand, it has considerable recommendations. Its society is larger and more varied than in any other station in the North-Western Provinces. Good, if expensive, houses can be got there. It has a most excellent club, and some beautiful gardens, which are being improved every year. Its great want is that it has none of the old native buildings for which Agra, Delhi, Lucknow, &c. are famous, and which are so beautiful. Lucknow, again, is a very large station—in fact, you may have to drive six or seven miles to call on people in it—and I think opinion varies a good deal with regard to it; with some it is very popular, while with others it is just the reverse.

Until lately, Oudh was ruled by a chief commissioner of its own, and there was a very good Government House at Lucknow, which is the capital of the province, but recently Oudh has been tacked on to the North-Western Provinces, the Lieutenant-Governor of which spends a certain portion of each cold season at Lucknow. It has a very large garrison, and the society is consequently more military than civilian.

Meerut is, as a rule, a very popular station; for while there is no want of society there, the place is not straggling, and there is no difficulty in meeting your friends. It is generally looked upon as a very good place from which to get sport, and it has the advantage besides of not being far from several hill stations.

Umballa, too, is a favourite station, partly for itself, but chiefly on account of its proximity to Simla. This is principally a military station, and comparatively speaking a new one, for the barracks were laid out and built under the supervision of Lord Napier of Magdala when he was Executive Engineer there, between thirty and forty years ago. In Indian stations, the portions where the military live are called the cantonments, while those occupied by the civilians are called the civil lines, and the proximity of the two varies much in different places. At Umballa, the principal part of the station—that is to say, where the large majority of houses are, also all the shops and hotels—is the cantonments; and the civil lines, where the civil officers chiefly live, are three miles away, close to the city.

This is another peculiarity of Indian stations, that they mostly have close to them large towns (always called cities), consisting of houses closely packed together, only separated by very narrow streets, and inhabited by thousands of natives. The fact is, that the cities existed long before the cantonments, the latter having been built as the country has been over-run and occupied by the British. The cities are generally under the control of municipal committees, which are chiefly managed by the civil authorities, and with which the military have nothing to do; while the cantonments with all the bazaars situated in them are entirely under the management of the military. It will frequently be found that the civil lines are close to the city, as it is most convenient for the civil officers to live near the people with whom they are chiefly concerned. And to take the case of Lahore. It is really a station by itself; the Lieutenant-Governor of the Punjab, with his secretaries, and the chief court judges, &c., living there; while Meean Meer, which is the military station or cantonment of Lahore, is four miles distant from it. I daresay I shall later on have more to say about various stations in India, but I would turn now to the subject of settling down in the country, and the first thing to do is to get a house.

It must be borne in mind that, except in the presidency towns of Calcutta, Madras, and Bombay, there are no such things as lodgings in India. There are certainly hotels in the larger stations, but these are mostly used only temporarily, and practically everyone makes up his mind that he must have a house. Bachelors as a rule join together in different numbers to take houses, and a bachelor coming out from England alone may find a friend quite willing to give him accommodation. But still everyone has to get a house in some shape or another, and I would say at once that, in settling down, there is nothing of greater importance than securing a good one, for it is a matter in which people are too apt to indulge in false economy.

I have already said that the rupee is supposed to represent two shillings, so to convert rupees into pounds it is only necessary to cut off the 0 at the end of the sum. Houses in the plains are always let by the month, and you will find people for the sake of saving twenty or thirty rupees a month (aye, and where the saving is of no absolute necessity either), taking a bad house instead of a good one. They overlook the fact that, if their bad house induces serious illness which drives them to England, even if it does not kill them outright, their economy will be a very poor one. No; you may take it for granted that the first thing to do is to get the best house, as far as health is concerned, that you can possibly afford. You will be able to see for yourself whether the house is well situated and likely to be on well-drained ground, &c. while a visit to it will probably inform you as to its ventilation. Besides this, you can make inquiries, from which you will be able to learn what reputation it bears as regards healthiness, coolness, &c.

There is by no means a superabundance of houses in most Indian stations, and though it is not generally difficult to get one of some sort, it is very likely that you may not be able to get at once exactly what you would wish, and in this case the only thing to do is to secure the refusal of some house that would suit you in case it might be vacant before you leave the station. Houses differ very much in temperature, and though a difference of three or four degrees in the thermometer does not sound much, it means more than people living in England can suppose. The difference is very often due to the roofing, which is of two kinds, either thatched or flat masonry—*pucca*, as it is called in Hindustani. There is no doubt that the thatched houses are much the coolest, and the chief thing against them is the possibility of their catching fire, but this very rarely occurs, and there is not often a fire in use to give rise to the danger. Perhaps, in December, January, and February, a fire may be lighted in the drawing-room in the evenings, but seldom more than this; and, personally, I must say, I should always run the remote risk of being burnt out, and choose a thatched house, on account of its greater coolness in summer. It is wonderful how soon one gets accustomed to the heat. In England, I have gone into a green-house, which felt suffocatingly hot, and on looking at the thermometer, found that the temperature was only between seventy degrees and eighty degrees. In India you would think your house perfectly cool at that, and punkahs are not often used till the thermometer has got past eighty-three or eighty-four degrees.

Having chosen your house, the next thing to do is to furnish it, as all houses in the plains are let absolutely bare of any furniture whatever, and this is not such an easy matter as dwellers in England might suppose. There are no upholsterers except in the presidency towns, and, even were they more accessible, their prices are prohibitive to most people. The system is for people to sell to each other. When anyone is leaving a station, either to return to England or on transfer to some other station, he makes out a list of what he does not wish to retain, with the price noted against each article. This list is then taken round by a servant from house to house, and those who want any of the articles contained in it put their names down against them. If the seller cannot dispose of all his property in this way, he probably has an auction of what remains, which is bought up at very low rates by the native shopkeepers, who buy the things in the hope that when some new comer is in want of furniture, they may be able to realize several cents. per cent. in relieving his necessity. If a new arrival happens to find one of these lists in circulation, he will probably be able to do a good deal towards fitting out his house, for houses in India are not nearly so elaborately furnished as those in England; but if not, he must get what is absolutely necessary from the natives in the bazaars, and then look out for opportunities, such as I have described, for completing his furnishing.

Houses in the hills are generally papered, but never in the plains. Here they have plastered walls, either white, or washed over with some tinted wash, and darker coloured lines are painted round the edges, with patterns of flowers or something of that sort at the corners. The first thing always done is to cover the floors, which are of plaster and not of wood, completely with coarse matting, over which is placed either finer matting, carpets, or, more usually, what are called *dhurries*. These are a sort of drugget made entirely of cotton, and are about the cheapest covering that can be used for floors in India. They are to be bought of different sizes and patterns in the bazaars, but the best I have ever seen are those made in the jails, and if the furnisher cannot pick up one that suits him, his best plan will be to order one from the nearest jail, for in the first place it will be made to any size he may wish, and, in the next, the jails have much nicer patterns, and are much more careful in their manufacture than the ordinary weavers are.

Carpets are better suited for furnishing houses

in the hills than in the plains, as in the latter they look too hot, and would, moreover, probably be soon destroyed by white ants. It is a very difficult matter to keep one's house clear of these insects, and if they once get in, they will make short work of anything except china or metal. There is one particular matting, though, which they will not touch, called *moonj* matting, and this is very useful for putting down in halls—I was going to add "and staircases," forgetting to mention that no houses in the plains, except in the presidency towns, and but very few in the hills, have any rooms upstairs. Nothing is nicer for floors in the plains than fine matting, which can be got from Calcutta, but it is expensive, and does not wear very well. If carpets are wanted, very nice ones can be got at Mirzapore, made to order. They are extremely handsome, wear very well, and cost about five rupees per square yard, which is, of course, dear compared to those made at home, but they will wear out two or three English carpets. I have noticed that the sale of them in London has evidently been increasing considerably of late. Still more elaborate ones are made in the jails, and amongst them the Lahore jail is noted for its manufacture; but if I remember aright, all the carpets made there are ten rupees per square yard, and a purchaser would have to wait a long time before he would get a carpet from Lahore, as they always have a number of orders registered, both from England and America. Notwithstanding their high prices, I do not suppose the Lahore jail would be able to supply a private individual with a carpet under two or three years. When dances are given on these plastered floors, the plan adopted is to stretch canvas cloths tightly over them, which, being well waxed, make very good floors for dancing on. Their chief failing is, that they have not the elasticity of boarded floors, and consequently are more tiring.

I should mention that there are some places where furniture is better made and more easily bought than others. Bareilly, for instance, in the North-West Provinces, is noted for the furniture turned out there by the native carpenters. They work slowly, as all natives do, but their work is well finished, and they use good and well-seasoned wood, the consequence being that orders for furniture are frequently sent to Bareilly from considerable distances.

While furnishing his house, the new arrival will also be completing his establishment of servants, which entails getting a considerable number, as they will not do two or three different sorts of work, as servants will do in England. First, as regards cooks. The best in the country are known as *mugs*, and come from Chittagong and the district round it on the Bay of Bengal. Why these men should be the best, I cannot say, but they are, and they get all the best paid service in Calcutta. At Government House, the head is almost always a French cook, but the four next to him are *mugs*, and very good cooks they are. They are not easy to get out of Calcutta, and are besides very expensive, their wages ranging from forty rupees a month down to about twenty, which are enormous for Oriental servants. However, the only thing to do is to examine a cook's characters, and take him if he seems likely to do, changing him if on trial he is found not to suit.

One hint I would give to housekeepers, which is either to visit the kitchen daily, and see that it has been properly cleaned out, or never go near it at all. Anyone who has been accustomed to a nice cleanly-kept English kitchen, would be horrified at what she would see in her new home, and really, unless prepared to exercise an amount of energy which it is very difficult after some stay in India to find available, it is best to eat what is put before one, asking no questions, unless such a glaring case of uncleanliness comes under one's notice that it is impossible to overlook it.

There is one thing that needs care, which is to ensure the cooking-utensils being tinned regularly twice a month, as they are all made of copper, and unless this is done you are very likely to find yourself poisoned in a more or less serious degree. Besides this, it is necessary to see that the tinning used is pure, for the natives are very fond of using stuff with a great deal of lead in it, which is nearly as dangerous as the verdigris on the copper. Of course the cook ought to attend to all this, but if you trust to what Indian servants *ought* to do, you will frequently find yourself in awkward difficulties.

People with large establishments have *khansamahs*, who occupy somewhat the same position that the housekeeper does in England. They are really the head of all the servants, issuing orders to the others, and they are responsible for the manufacture of all the sweets, cakes, puddings, preserves, &c. The bearer is really the valet, taking charge of his master's clothes, &c., while the care and management of all the lamps fall also to his lot.

There are certain places which are noted for

supplying the best servants of different classes. For instance, Furruckabad always used to be the great place for bearers, Lucknow for *kitmutgars* (table attendants), and Meerut for *dirzees* (tailors). In former days people used to put the greatest trust in their bearers, making over to them all their keys, money up to, perhaps, some thousands of rupees, and, in a word, all their possessions. Very faithfully, too, these men fulfilled their trust, but, for some reason or another, I do not think this system prevails now as much as it used to do. I suppose this arises from altered circumstances, perhaps from the more frequent visits to England, which would entail the more frequent change in servants; but whatever the cause, there is certainly, I think, a difference. You will also find people, especially if they are not well off, rolling up the bearer and kitmutgar into one, and this brings us to the consideration of the latter. These are the footmen, waiting at table, cleaning the plate (or rather not cleaning it, for I hardly ever saw plate decently cleaned in India yet), and such like. Besides this, as I have said, they very often do bearers' work as well, and then only resemble their prototype in England, who combines the duties of valet and footman.

In addition a *mussalchi* will be required, who acts as scullery-maid, and does all the washing-up. They kill all the poultry used in the kitchen, and very brutal they often are at this work. It seems hardly credible, but there is a theory amongst native servants that the only way to kill a turkey properly is to tear its tongue out and then leave it to bleed to death! Directly I found this out I gave orders that all the poultry, both turkeys and fowls, used in my house were to be killed by having their heads chopped off at a single blow, which is infinitely the more merciful way of putting an end to them, and took care to ensure the orders being adhered to. If anyone in India who may happen to read this paper gives similar orders, it will not have been written in vain.

Besides these servants every house has its own *dhoby*, or washerman, and I may here mention that, with the exception of ayahs who perform the duties of nurses or ladies' maids, all servants in India are men. *Dhobies* vary a good deal, but some of them wash very well, though they knock one's things to pieces a good deal, as washing is usually done by beating the clothes on a board or stone in a running stream; still it is a great comfort to know that the man is at your beck and call, that you have only to send out to him whatever you want washed or ironed, and that it will be done at once.

Another indispensable servant is the sweeper, or, as he is often called, "the Knight of the Broom." He sweeps out all the rooms in the house, empties slops, &c. while the bearer does the dusting. Hindoo servants are of different castes, but the sweeper is the lowest of all. He, for instance, will eat the leavings from his master's table, while a Hindoo of a higher caste would not so much as touch the plate or dish containing them.

The *bheesty*, or water-carrier, provides the water-supply, as you very rarely see such things as pipes and taps, and he does this in the plains by drawing water from wells and filling his *mussuck*, which he then carries slung from one shoulder. The *mussuck* is made from the skin of a goat, which is taken off whole, when it is sewn up and greased till it is pretty well waterproof. In the hills water is usually collected from springs, but at Simla there is a supply brought by pipes from about six miles off, and laid on all over the station, the *bheesties* filling their *mussucks* at the various taps. *Bheesties*, I think, are noted for being more faithful and giving less trouble than any of the servants. Of course carrying water is not a very difficult duty to perform, but *bheesties* are usually ready to do whatever they are wanted, and to turn their hands to anything which does not affect their religion, and they are noted for having been specially faithful to us in the Mutiny. Troops when on the march, when on field days in sham, or in action in earnest, are always accompanied by *bheesties*, and dozens of stories are told of how, during the Mutiny, they went anywhere and under any fire, to give our wounded soldiers water.

Another servant that is generally required, certainly in a house where there are any children, is a *dirzee* or tailor, for, as I have said, *ayahs* know nothing of needlework, and the *dirzees* do all the making and mending which in England would be done by ladies' maids or nurses. These *dirzees* are wonderful fellows: not one in a thousand knows anything of measuring, but give them a pattern, and they will copy it most exactly.

Altogether it will be seen that the house servants are numerous, and they vary in number according to the position and means of the owner. I would now make one remark, which is, that it is a great mistake not to treat your servants kindly. The reader who knows nothing of India says, no doubt, "Why should I treat them unkindly?" But, in truth, there are many things out there to try the temper and make people less patient than they are in England. Ill health, which is not unfrequent, the heat, the lying and perhaps cheating of servants, and very often their dirty habits, render it very difficult always to keep the temper. But individual characters very soon become known all through the bazaars, and the best servants invariably go to those who have the reputation of being the best masters.

It is hardly possible to expect an Oriental always to speak the truth, but the less your servant fears you the more ready will he be to speak it; and as regards cheating, there is one way in which the servant always makes a profit at the cost of the master, and which is generally recognised as legitimate. This is by taking from all native shopkeepers *dustooree*, which translated means "custom," and corresponds to "perquisites" in English. The rule is for the shopkeeper to pay one anna in the rupee (or one-sixteenth of the rupee) to the servant who purchases the goods, and of course the tradesman takes care that the loss does not fall on him, but on the purchaser, fixing the price of his goods with this view.

Besides the house-servants, there are those for out-door work to be provided, and first for the stables. Riding and driving are not luxuries in India—they are necessities, and everyone has to keep a conveyance of some sort. In England one man is supposed to look after two horses. In the East it is just the reverse, and there are two servants to each horse. One is the *syce* or groom, the other is the grass-cutter.

I should explain that in most parts of India there is no such thing as hay. The grass-cutters go out daily, grubbing up the grass which they find in fields or by the roadside, and making it up into bundles. It is poor-looking stuff, but still it is wonderful how the horses and ponies thrive on it. The *syce* always stays at home, grooming his horse, cleaning harness, and so forth, ready to saddle the horse and accompany his master if he wants to go out; for people riding short distances, that is to say, about stations, &c., always take their *syces* with them to hold their horses while they are dismounted.

There is one peculiarity about *syces* in Bengal, which is that when out at exercise they never ride but always lead the horses. In Mádras and Bombay they ride much more.

If you wish to have decent milk and butter it is essential to keep cows, for it is impossible to buy good butter in the bazaars, and very hard to get good milk. It is not, as a rule, difficult to get cows of some sort or another, though you may not be able to pick up at once just what you would wish.

A cow is said to give so many *seers* of milk a day, the *seer* being almost the exact equivalent of a quart. The generality of them only yield about five *seers* a day, and though they differ in this respect, it is a very first-rate one that gives as much as ten *seers*. They are naturally not nearly so expensive as cows in England, and the usual price is about five or six rupees per *seer*; that is to say, the price of a cow which gives six *seers* of milk will be from thirty to thirty-six rupees. For an extraordinarily good animal the rate I have mentioned would probably be raised, and one giving ten *seers* of milk would fetch seventy or eighty rupees. It is only right that this should be so, for, after all, the great expense of the cow is its keep, and a bad one eats just as much as a good one does. If you keep cows there must be a man to look after them, and he is called a *gowalla*.

Most people keep a few goats, also, for the sake of their milk, which is drunk quite fresh with tea instead of cream; and I know few better things than a cup of really good Indian hill tea, with milk just drawn from the goat poured foaming into it.

Then there is the garden to be attended to. Every compound has a garden of some sort in it, and to say nothing of maintaining the neatness of the place, and the pleasure of having the flowers, it is essential to keep up a garden for the sake of the vegetables. The gardeners are called *malis*; and though some of them—owing to the instructions they have received from their masters—are better than others, it is not easy to get a man who really knows much of his business. In the plains the great time for the garden is during the cold weather, for in the hot weather everything is dried up, and this period really corresponds to the winter in England. You can produce almost any sort of vegetable; and while some of them, with care, can be grown just as good as in England, it seems impossible to get the proper flavour into others. Celery, beetroot, lettuces, radishes, onions, cabbages, cauliflowers, and turnips, are all that can be desired; while though you may grow carrots, peas, French beans, or broad beans, they never taste as they ought to do. Potatoes can be grown in the plains, but they do much better in the hills, and those raised there are as fine as anyone can wish for.

It must not be supposed that an Indian garden can compare with an English one. It is true that you have plants, which can only be reared in hot-houses in England, growing almost as bushes in the open air in India—such, for instance, are the *gardenia*, *poinsettia*, and *bougainvillia*—but the absence of the smooth green turf and the evergreens which are always such beautiful features in an English garden is a serious drawback, and cannot in my opinion be made up for in other ways. Some of the public gardens, such as those in Calcutta, Lucknow, Allahabad, Agra, and Umritsur, are beautifully kept up, and have large sums of money spent on them; but I cannot help thinking that owing to the difference in gardens and climate, a similar outlay would produce better results in England. Roses do very well in India, and during the cold weather there is always a magnificent show to be seen in the Taj' gardens at Agra.

The fruit is not to be compared to that in England. Peaches are tolerably good. Grapes are grown on vineries made of rows of brick pillars with wooden framework laid on them to support the trees; but the fruit produced is only like that grown on walls in England, and very much inferior to hot-house grapes. Apples, pears, currants, raspberries, gooseberries, &c. do not grow at all in the plains, but I have seen fine pears and apples grown from English stocks in the hills; while in a few instances people who have been settled in the Himalayas for some years, cultivate their English fruit with very tolerable success. Mangoes yield the chief fruit-harvest of India, and are very nice for a time, but I think one soon gets tired of them, and the melons which grow profusely in the hot weather are by no means bad. Cashmere is the best place in India for fruit, and just outside our frontier the Afghans are very successful in their gardening. At Cabul I have seen beautiful grapes of various sorts, peaches, apricots, cherries, apples, and pears, the fact being that these fruits do better in the more temperate climate.

I have spoken about the stable-servants who will be required, but I have as yet said nothing about the horses that are to be got in the country. English horses are very rare, and only to be found when they have been taken out by people for their own special use. Those that can generally be purchased are of three descriptions, viz. Arabs, which are mostly landed at Bombay and thence distributed up country; Australians, generally called "Walers," because they come from New South Wales; and "country-breds," or the horses bred in India. There is no doubt that a really fine Arab is a very pleasant horse to ride. As a rule they are first-rate in their canter and gallop, but it is very difficult to find one that trots well, and generally difficult to find one that walks well.

If you can secure one that is good in all his paces, no horse is better suited for India than the Arab.

The "Waler" is altogether much more like the English horse (and naturally so as he is bred from English stock) both in make, shape, and paces. They, too, very often fail in that most essential quality of walking well, and chiefly, I fancy, because they have never had any experience of the deep heavy ground there is in England, which compels a horse to pick up his feet and bend his knees. Formerly it was very difficult to get quiet "Walers." Many of them were given to buck-jumping, a habit contracted, I daresay, because, from the large number of animals to be broken in Australia and the very few rough-riders to do it, the latter could not afford to give the time and attention necessary to break a young horse well and carefully. There is a great improvement in this respect, and many of the horses landed at Calcutta from Australia are perfectly well broken, and very fine animals into the bargain. I cannot say that I am very fond of the "country-bred" myself. They are, of course, a great deal used, and especially for harness, as they are by far the cheapest horses in the country, but it is very seldom that they fail to betray their origin in some way sooner or later. You may be riding or driving along quietly, when your horse suddenly stands stock-still and refuses to move. If you try to get him forward, up he goes straight on end. It simply arises from a bit of hereditary sulkiness or obstinacy, and may fairly be called "the mark of the beast." However, in purchasing horses, as in everything else, the new comer will have to be guided by his tastes, wants, and, last but not least, by his means. India is like most other countries, it has no lack of good horses for those who are able to pay for them. Most people going out take a saddle and some bridles with them, but there are frequent opportunities for buying such things, when necessary, from those who have more than they want, or are leaving the country.

The new arrival is now supposed to be settled down in his bungalow, servants engaged, horses, &c. bought, and his whole establishment in working order, so we may now look at what life in a plains' station generally is through the year. We will suppose the time to be towards the end of October, when the hot weather is pretty well over, and the climate becoming pleasanter every day. *Punkahs* are being taken down and put away, and people are preparing to spend a pleasant six months, for there is no doubt that the cold weather in India is enjoyable enough. During the summer there is not only the heat to be borne, but life in the plains is very dull, because all who can do so escape to the hill stations; but in the winter almost all the houses are occupied, people are constantly meeting each other, and there are lawn tennis or afternoon parties of some sort every day. Dinner parties, picnics, and dances, too, are not infrequent, and life passes away pleasantly enough. Shooting begins now, and though I do not wish to write much on a subject which easily might and often has filled volumes, I would just say sufficient to indicate the seasons for the different sorts of game. For instance, the autumn is not the time for big game shooting. The rains have only lately ceased, and owing to them and the hot-house heat, the heavy jungles where tigers, &c. are to be found have become so dense that it would be impossible to beat them. I have been shooting in December from an elephant's back in the Terai, which runs under the Himalayas, where the grass was over my head as I was standing up, and this would make it from sixteen to seventeen feet high. Besides this, the jungles are so feverish and unhealthy after the rains, that they can really only be called deadly until the dampness has dried up and they are once more safe to sleep in, which is hardly before December. But snipe and duck are beginning to come down from the north in October, and towards the end of that month very good sport can be got, which goes on improving till the following spring, when the birds disappear with the increasing heat.

There are marshes, or *jheels*, as they are called, which can be reached from most stations, and as a rule they afford first-rate sport. It is wonderful how soon one gets rid of two or three hundred cartridges, and thirty or forty couple of snipe is no unusual bag for one gun. Besides these, there are various kinds of partridge to be got, but they are terrible birds to run, and their flavour is so indifferent that they are hardly worth eating when killed. There are generally two or three hares to be seen in a day's shooting, but rabbits do not exist at all in India. Then, for those who like deer-stalking, there are very often antelope, or, as they are called, black buck, to be got within a ride, and, in fact, the real sportsman will hardly ever be at a loss for amusement. As the spring comes on, and the burning sun dries up the grass, the time for tiger-shooting approaches. I am speaking now more particularly of the Terai, which stretches away in a belt for many miles along the base of the Himalayas. Here, when the grass is sufficiently dry, the cowherds set fire to it, and over the burnt-up remains the young grass springs up, on which their cattle feed. There are left here and there patches of grass, which are generally full of deer of different sorts, while an occasional tiger may be found in the heavier coverts, through which, perhaps, a stream passes.

I know few things more delightful in the shooting line than to be out in the jungle about the end of March, with four or five pleasant companions and about five-and-twenty elephants. You get into the howdah after breakfast, shoot all day, stopping for luncheon, and either return in the evening to the camp from which you started, or find it moved to some fresh spot, whence on the morrow you will beat new ground. The sport, the scenery, and the complete absence of all official work and cares, combine to make the holiday perfect, and there is nothing but regret when the trip is over and the camp has to be abandoned for the station. The only thing against this mode of shooting is its expense. Elephants are costly animals to feed, and a party going out on a sporting trip always takes care to live pretty comfortably; the result probably being rather a high bill at the end of the expedition.

Tiger-shooting is not what it used to be, at any rate in our Terai. Cultivation has increased so much, that the jungles are considerably diminished in extent, and tigers are not so numerous as they were. The way to see tiger-shooting from elephants in perfection, is to get an invitation to join some party going into the Nepal Terai. There the jungles still exist in all their primeval grandeur, and you may almost say that tigers are preserved. No party ever goes there without killing several, while in our own districts you may beat for days and kill only one or two, or, perhaps, none. I am not at all arguing that jungles or tigers should be maintained for sport; I am only saying what is the actual state of the case.

Tiger-shooting is carried on without elephants in a great many parts of India, and the regiment known as the Central India Horse, for instance, organise shooting-parties, which, I think, go on through May and June, where elephants are hardly used at all. On one point there can be no doubt, which is that India is the country for a man who is fond of shooting, and who has no friend to give it him in England.

It might, perhaps, be useful to say here a few words regarding the weapons which anyone intending to shoot should take out with him, and my first advice on this head is not to be in a hurry. Let everyone take out what he has, but unless the sportsman is a person in easy circumstances, and only going to India for a sporting trip, I think he would do well to wait till he gets out and has time to see what he will want. It may be that he will find himself in a station near which there is no game for a rifle, and his duties may be such that he will for a time be unable to get away on leave. Then, different sorts of rifles are required for different sorts of game. For black buck shooting, there is nothing like the express, while for howdah shooting or jungle shooting, where game passes rapidly and close to you, people differ in their opinions as to what is the best style of rifle to have. Myself, shooting from the howdah, I prefer a double-barrelled snider-bore to anything. You can buy as many of the cartridges, all ready made up, from the Government magazines as you choose; the bullet inflicts a frightful wound, and the charge of powder being comparatively small, there is not the jar which is experienced in firing the Express or 12-bore, which take four or five drams of powder.

People may fancy that in large game shooting you do not get many shots in the course of the day; but when the jungle is burnt, the patches which are left are often full of deer, and at certain times you are blazing away as fast as you can load. I remember on one occasion firing away one hundred and thirty cartridges loaded with four and a half drams of powder in the course of the day, the result being that at the end I felt as though my head would burst, and had the most frightful headache.

There is another thing to be borne in mind. As in the case of saddlery and harness, either because they are going to England, or for some other reason, people are constantly selling their guns and rifles, and any sportsman wishing to fit himself out will find advertisements every day in the local papers from which to choose, and if he looks out he will probably be able to get the style of weapon he wants, perfectly good and much cheaper than if he had bought it new in London.

Besides game-shooting, there is no lack of amusement for the target-shot. Every presidency has its rifle association, and as the meetings are held at different seasons of the year, anyone who is keen on the subject can attend them all, if he can only command the necessary leisure.

The cold weather, also, is the time for hunting. This cannot in any way be compared with that in England. At some few places draft fox-hounds or harriers are got out from England, and packs organised; but there is a great deal against hunting. In the first place, there is no animal to hunt like the fox. The jackal has to take his place, but he is not the same thing either for pluck or endurance. Then scent is a great difficulty. The only way to secure any at all, is to commence hunting as soon it is day-light; for directly the sun gets up, the scent disappears entirely, and it is hopeless to try and get any. Peshawar has always been considered the best place, at any rate in Upper India, for hunting, partly, I suppose, because from its northern latitude it has the longest and the coldest winter, and perhaps, also, the valley in which it lies may be somewhat damper, and consequently retains scent better than other places.

Another thing which causes some trouble and expense is that the hounds must always be sent up to the hills in the hot weather, or they would inevitably die. The country too, is not the same thing to ride over as in England. There are, properly speaking, hardly any fences, the only obstacles as a rule being ditches, with, perhaps, a mud wall here and there. I think the most popular sport in India in the hunting line, if it can so be called, is pig-sticking; but there are not many places from which this can be got.

I will not enter into any detail of how pig-sticking is managed, because it is not my object to write an essay on sport, but to give a general idea of life in India throughout the year.

For fishing the country is, I should say, decidedly badly off. There are rivers where *mahseer* can be caught, and very large ones too, but it is not easy to get them to take a fly, and the usual method is spoon bait or artificial bait of some sort. They run up to a very considerable size, and fight well when hooked, but if over six or seven pounds in weight they are very coarse for eating. Personally, I do not think any of the fresh-water fish in India worth anything for the table. They are all very bony and tasteless, the consequence being that when people give dinner-parties they almost always use tinned English fish. Down in the Central Provinces there are what they call trout, but they share the peculiarity of their Indian brethren in being bony and comparatively tasteless. The fresh-water fish mostly used for the table are called *ruh*, but they are entirely taken with the net. Altogether, fish is a great want in India, certainly for sport, but more especially for food. As regards salt-water fish, the *hilsa* at Calcutta and the *pomfret* or *pomphlet* at Bombay are very good, but there is nothing like the variety that we have in England.

Anyone who cares about hawking can have

ample opportunity for practising it. In almost every city there are two or three men who are accustomed to it, and train hawks, while the birds themselves abound all over the country.

I do not think I need say anything more about sport properly so called, but may return to life in the station and the amusements there.

Cricket is hardly played at all except during the cold weather, but wherever there are Englishmen you will find the national game, and matches are frequent throughout the winter. One of the most popular games is polo, and India gives unusual facilities for this. As I have said, riding there is not a luxury, but a necessity. Everyone keeps a pony or two, and consequently can, if he likes, easily fit himself out for polo. Then, again, the country abounds with ponies, most of which can be got at moderate prices, instead of costing the fabulous sums that are given for really good polo ponies in England, so that there is nothing to prevent anyone who likes it from taking part in the game. Almost every station has one or more racquet courts, which are chiefly used during the hot weather, as this is much the most suitable time for playing. They differ from those in England in that they are almost always open or uncovered courts, while the balls used in play are black instead of being white. Lawn tennis is a game which has become exceedingly popular in India, and is wonderfully well adapted to the country. The compounds surrounding houses give ample space for courts, which are almost always of mud. Turf grows so badly and is so difficult to keep in proper order, that much the simplest plan is to have the coarse grass peeled off, and the ground then watered, hammered, and rolled, when it gives as good a surface for lawn tennis as could possibly be desired.

And so life goes on in the Indian station. To the civilians, in some ways, the season of the year does not make very much difference, for he always has his hands pretty full in doing his magisterial work, the only difference being that in the summer he commences about 6 A.M., closing his court at noon, while in the winter he begins at about 11 A.M. and ends at 6 P.M. During the cold weather, all the civilians except the judges are a great deal out in camp, as their districts have to be visited, revenue collected, and many things attended to which could not possibly be done without personal supervision. I suppose the world does not contain a body of men who work harder than the Indian civilians do. They are highly paid, but not more highly than they deserve, and considering what they have to go through to get their posts, and the amount of work expected from them when appointed, it is only right that they should be well paid.

India has a precedence list of its own, according to which civilians rank very much higher than the military. For instance, a civilian, by which I mean a member of the Indian Civil Service, ranks with a captain, who, by the Staff

Corps rules, cannot attain that position under twelve years' service; a civilian of eight years' service with a major who has twenty; and a civilian of twelve with a lieutenant-colonel who has twenty-six years' service. Rank, which would take precedence in England, is of no account whatever in India; and this, no doubt, is right enough, but I do not quite see why the civilians should be placed so far above the military, who are really the people that hold the country. Sweep the former away, and amongst the latter you could find men to carry on the business of the Empire, for many of the most eminent Indian administrators have been soldiers; but take away the army, and where would the civilians be?

There is a sort of idea amongst people, or at any rate some people, in England, that society in India is of the most indifferent sort, that very queer things go on there, and that altogether it is quite below the level of that in England. A greater mistake there could not be. Indian society contains as pleasant and well-informed people as any other does, while, as for kindliness and hospitality, I defy the world to beat it. In the Indian Civil Service there are many men of remarkable power and ability; while as far as the army is concerned, India will compare favourably with any part of the British possessions, for it is *par excellence* the country for soldiering. As regards morality generally, I do not mean to say that India is blameless, and I should like to be shown the country that is; but I suspect it would compare favourably with England.

I need hardly say that the postal and telegraph services are well carried out all over the country. There is scarcely a station, however small, that is without its telegraph office, and the uniform rate for telegraphing, all over India, is one rupee for six words, not including the address. The various stations, too, are as a rule very well off for churches. Almost all of them have good and large ones, while some of them are remarkably fine buildings. Those at Umballa, Meean Meer, and Peshawar are, I should say, specially worthy of remark, while some have been built as memorials of the Mutiny, as at Futtehgurh and Cawnpore, which would be considered fine churches anywhere. The services are suited to the climate, and not so long as those in England; for instance, Morning Prayer and the Litany are never given at the same service, but are generally read on alternate Sundays. The singing, as a rule, is not quite worthy of the churches; but there are great difficulties about this. There is rarely anything but a harmonium, and even where there is an organ it is often difficult to find anyone to play it. Then there is no supply of boys to fill up the choir as there is in England, and when a clergyman has to depend solely on amateurs the outlook for his choir is not a very good one. If the material were available, I do not think there would be any difficulty about raising the money to pay for it, as there are collections after every service, while people are in easier circumstances and more beyond that constant feeling of want of money which is so common in England, and so depressing to those who suffer from it. One peculiarity about the country is that people hardly ever carry money in their pockets except when travelling, and this difficulty is met in church by sending round in the plates packets of cards on which donors write down what they wish to give. The cards are then taken to the various houses during the week, and the donations written on them are paid up.

There is another story told of Bishop Wilson on this very subject. He was preaching in the Cathedral at Calcutta, and in the course of his sermon commented on the difficulty there very often was in collecting the sums which had been written down on the cards. He said: "When the *chuprassies* [servants employed on messenger work] go to your houses, some say '*Kul ao*' [Come to-morrow]; and some say '*Parson ao*' [Come the day after to-morrow];

and some—oh! the wickedness of this world—say '*Jehannum ko jao*.'" When I say that *jao* means "go," *ko* "to," and that *Jehannum* corresponds to Gehenna, I do not think that I need explain any further what the worthy bishop complained of.

The spiritual wants of the European community are attended to by five bishops, five archdeacons, ninety Church of England chaplains in Bengal, and, I think, about forty each in the Madras and Bombay Presidencies. Besides these, there are Roman Catholic and Presbyterian chaplains. Formerly there were only three bishoprics, viz. Calcutta, Madras, and Bombay, but these have been lately increased by two more, Lahore and Burmah; and it was not before they were wanted, for it must always have been a mystery how the Bishop of Calcutta, for instance, got through his work. I have frequently rather wondered why Church of England chaplaincies in India are not more sought after, for as a rule the work is very light compared to an English living or curacy, and the pay by no means bad.

The clergy are divided into two classes; junior and senior chaplains. The former receive five hundred rupees per mensem till they have completed ten years' service, when they are raised to eight hundred rupees per mensem, and this does not include any time spent on furlough. After a total service of seventeen years, which must be exclusive of furlough, the chaplain can, if he pleases, retire to England on a pension of one pound a day for the rest of his life; not a bad addition to any other employment he may be able to obtain there. Or he can, if he pleases, hold on till he has completed twenty-five years' service, when he is obliged to retire on the pension I have mentioned. His work in India is not hard, and there is none of the visiting in slums which has to be gone through in the towns of England. The poor part, so to say, of his congregation is almost entirely composed of British soldiers and a few pensioners, the former of whom he has to visit in barracks and hospitals, the latter in their own homes; while if he is not at all times a welcome guest in pleasant society it is his own fault.

Besides the advantages I have mentioned, every chaplain, if he wishes it, is pretty sure of at least two tours of duty at a hill station, each tour lasting two years, while there are always the archdeaconries as prizes to be obtained, with much higher pay and retiring pensions than the chaplaincies, though the five are not all on quite the same scale.

The clergy are paid for out of the Government revenues on the ground that they are required for the soldiers, and they consequently have nothing to do with the natives. These are entirely attended to by missionaries of various nationalities, of whom I think I am justified in saying that by far the larger proportion are American Dissenters, who are also trained as doctors, and thus combine the cure of the body with that of the soul. To say that they are thoroughly earnest, hard-working men, does not give much idea of all they go through in the profession they have adopted; but as far as conversions go, I fear they are not very successful. Such firmly established religions as Mohammedanism and Hindooism are not easily upset, but at any rate the missionaries of all nations have done a vast deal of good by the education they have diffused through the country, and this, I think, is the object they chiefly aim at.

To those who are fond of the stage India is certainly disappointing, for there is little to be seen there in the way of professional theatricals. There are generally companies in the presidency towns during the cold weather, and some of them occasionally take trips round to various stations, but I am afraid these journeys do not as a rule pay very well. There have been opera companies occasionally at Calcutta in the winter, but, I suppose, owing to the increased cost of living, and the loss by exchange to which I have referred, it is found to be more and more difficult to raise the necessary subscriptions to keep them afloat, and I do not think there has been any opera for some seasons past now.

As the winter passes by and April draws near, the increasing heat tells of the approaching migration to the hills, when their season commences, and plains' stations lead a life of dreary quietude till the heat once more disappears. For the military part of society the leave-season is from the 15th April till the 15th October, and between these dates most officers take it in turns to leave their regiments and go to the hills, while some people, both military and civilian, hold appointments which take them up there for the whole of the hot weather. Others, again, go for six months to Cashmere, and there are few pleasanter ways of spending the summer; in a splendid climate, amidst magnificent scenery, and with, generally speaking, good shooting. Another thing which recommends Cashmere to many officers is, that while there they draw pay at the Indian rate. If they took six months' leave to England, not only would there be the expense of the passage home and back, but while away they would only receive English pay. The official reason for this is that in Cashmere the officer is actually in India, and, therefore, can easily be recalled if required. But as a matter of fact the probabilities are that he could rejoin more speedily from England. A telegram to any address there would bring him out in three weeks; while a letter sent into Cashmere (for there is no telegraph beyond our own territory) might not find him for weeks if he were somewhere out in the wilds shooting, and under any circumstances he would hardly be likely to rejoin under a month.

Those who are not fortunate enough to get away make preparations for resisting the heat as well as they can, and the first thing to do is to have the *punkahs* put up ready for use as soon as the thermometer rises to 84° or 85°. Without these life would be unendurable. They keep one cool, keep off the flies, and, in fact, under the *punkah* is the only comfortable place in the hot weather. Without them, too, it would be absolutely impossible to sleep.

Another means of lowering the temperature usually adopted is by having *tatties* or screens of *khuskhus* grass fixed in the open doorways. About the beginning of May the hot winds commence blowing, and keep on more or less till the rains set in, which they do about the middle of June. When water is dashed over the screens so as to wet them thoroughly, the hot wind blows through them into the house quite cool, and sitting near a *tatty* is pleasant enough.

Another means of cooling the house is by machines called thermantidotes. A thermantidote is a large sort of box with a revolving fan inside, which is turned by coolies. On both sides of the box are apertures in which are fitted small *khuskhus tatties.* The machine has a mouth fitting into a door of the house constructed for the purpose. When the fan is turned on it drives the air through the mouth into the house, and as this becomes exhausted in the machine a fresh supply is drawn in through the *tatties*, which, being wetted, cool it. A good thermantidote will make a difference of 4° or 5° in the temperature of a room, and what that means only those who have lived in tropical climates can realise.

I laid great stress on the necessity of having a good house, and it is of no less importance to have the best food you can buy. Naturally in the hot weather there is not much inclination to eat, but whatever food you take should be the best you can get for money. About bread there is no difficulty; that can always be got good in every station, but meat is a very different matter. It is impossible to get good mutton in the bazaars, and the only plan is to belong to what is called a "mutton club"; that is to say, a certain number of people join together and keep a lot of sheep, which are fed on a grain called *gram*, and so many sheep are killed per week and divided according to the number of members in the club. A sheep should not be killed until it has been fed up for six months, but after that, if it is of the right kind and the proper age, it will be found to be very excellent mutton. Beef can be got pretty good in the bazaars, but even for that it is far better, if possible, to belong to what is called a "*gynee* club." *Gynees* are a small breed of cattle, and after being well fed turn into first-rate beef. Fowls and ducks are much cheaper than they are in England. Pig meat, such as pork and bacon, can hardly be obtained in India, and the bacon always used is that which comes out in tins from England.

One cannot avoid having a great many tinned things, owing to the difficulty of making up a really good dinner without them. For instance, at dinner-parties the fish would be tinned, the bacon, the *pâté de foie gras*, asparagus, and cheese, if all these things were used, and maybe others as well. A story is told of a lady who was born in India and had never been out of the country. She heard that a distinguished officer who had been home on leave had, while there, dined at Windsor Castle; so the first time she met him, she said, "I hear you dined with the Queen?" "Yes," he replied. "Ah! nothing but tinned provisions, I suppose?" said the lady, as this was her only idea of what a first-rate dinner could be!

Then ice is a matter of great importance in the hot weather; in fact, it makes all the difference between living a moderately comfortable life and simply existing. India is much better off in this respect than it used to be, as there are large establishments for the manufacture of ice by machinery in most parts of the country, and a station can hardly be so small or out of the way that people living in it cannot arrange to get machine-made ice from somewhere. In the upper parts of India there are, as a rule, several nights of frost in the course of the winter, and the plan (which is still adopted in some places) always used to be to put out an immense number of shallow earthen saucers, in which a little water was placed. These saucers are examined in the early morning, long before daylight, and if there has been a slight frost a very thin coating of ice is found on them. This is all carefully collected at once and carried away to the ice-pits, where it is tightly rammed down and kept for summer use. This is the cheapest ice, but it can only be used to put round bottles, while the machine ice, which is made in large slabs, can be broken up into lumps and put into wine or water. In the hills there are no ice-machines, and the plan there is to collect the snow which usually falls in the winter, ram it down tightly in pits, and then use it in the summer to put round bottles.

One thing, which is of great importance to those who wish to keep their health during the hot weather, is to be moderate about eating, drinking, and smoking. As I have said, the inclination to eat is usually not great, but drinking is quite another matter, and I think the experience of most people shows that for those who are not teetotallers the very light wines mixed with soda-water form about the best and safest beverages.

There are few things more refreshing or wholesome in the hot weather than lime-juice and soda-water. The limes are ripe a short time before the summer sets in, and it is very easy to get any number of them and save the juice, mixed with sugar, in bottles.

The summer in India, or the hot weather, as it is called in contradistinction to the cold weather, which is the term used for winter, has several phases. It sets in about the beginning of April in Upper India, and increases in severity till the middle of June, or whenever the rains commence, as this season varies in different parts of the country. As long as the dry heat lasts it is essential to keep the house closed, except for a short time in the middle of the night, when it is opened for the sake of ventilation. It is during these two months of dry heat that therm-antidotes are so useful, and the hot winds, which are like the sirocco, blow during the day-time, and, blowing through the wetted *khuskhus tatties*, cool the houses.

The only variations are occasional dust-storms, so called because of the violent gales of wind which raise vast clouds of dust, and darken the atmosphere almost as much as a London fog does. These storms cool the air somewhat for a short time, but the first real relief is experienced when the monsoon or rainy season sets in. Directly this takes place houses are thrown open at once for the sake of thorough ventilation, as *tatties* and thermantidotes are only of use in dry heat, and from the setting in of the monsoon till the end of the summer the heat is damp. The thermometer falls now considerably, but it is not wonderful that the weather, though less oppressive, is not nearly so healthy as it is during the dry heat. This is the great time of the year for fever, and it is almost always at this season that cholera claims its victims.

One can put up with a great deal if only a good night's rest can be secured, and during the dry heat I always found that the best plan was to have my bed put outside, and sleep out of doors. This can be done without a *punkah* long after it would be possible to do without one in the house, and when the heat increases so much as to render a *punkah* necessary even out of doors there is not much difficulty in fitting one up on a framework, but as soon as the rains set in sleeping out of doors is out of the question; for, even if it were not raining, the damp rising from the ground would be certain to produce fever. It is, of course, not astonishing that this is the time for the growth of vegetation. Between copious rainfall and hot-house heat, it would be wonderful were it otherwise; but it is not the time either for the flower or vegetable garden, as they only thrive during the cold weather. What I mean is that grass springs up rapidly, and attains a considerable height, while creepers, &c abound everywhere; and it is at this season that the jungles acquire that denseness which is only mown down by fire after several months of nearly uninterrupted dry weather.

During the two months of dry heat, those who are tied to the plains have to keep themselves shut up in their houses during the day. The early morning is the time to go out for a ride or drive, returning home by nine or half-past nine, and remaining under the *punkah* till about five o'clock in the afternoon, when people go out to racquets or lawn tennis, or whatever they may want to do.

During the rains they have more liberty, as it is frequently possible to be about out of doors all day long, but there is a greater feeling of languor, and I think most people would say that they enjoy better health and feel more fit either for work or amusement in the extreme but dry heat than they do when the rains have set in. The monsoon comes to an end about the middle of September, or earlier, according to the part of India in which you live, and then people who have been spending the summer in the plains begin to look forward to the return of their friends who have been fortunate enough to get to the hills, and to what is really the enjoyable time in the plains, viz. the cold weather. Of this I have spoken before, so I may consider that I have now given a slight idea of how the whole year passes in the plains, and will proceed to say a few words about life in the Indian hill-stations.

As regards Upper India, the principal of these, commencing northwards, are Murree, Dalhousie, Kasauli, Simla, Mussoorie, Naini Tal, and Darjeeling. There are others which are chiefly occupied by infantry regiments, but I need only speak of the larger ones, as my object is to show how society lives in our great eastern possession. They commence to fill about the beginning of April, and from that time till the middle of October, most houses in the various hill-stations are occupied. The localities are as a rule extremely pretty, with beautiful scenery and surroundings. The houses are built in all sorts of queer places; some on ridges, others on foundations cut out of the side of some hill, and I must confess that many of them look extremely insecure. However, they have stood for years, and unless overcome by some calamity like the great land-slip which occurred in Naini Tal in 1880, will, no doubt, stand for many more.

In Ootacamund, which is the hill-station for Madras, and a very beautiful one, too, I believe, people drive freely all over the place, but in most of those which I have mentioned in Upper India driving is impossible. Two or three people, such as the Viceroy and Commander-in-Chief, are allowed to have pony carriages in Simla; but as a rule, the means of locomotion in the hills is either by riding for men, or by *jampans* and *dandies* for ladies.

These are two sorts of chairs carried by coolies, who are called while hired for this purpose *jampannies*. The former requires four men at a time to carry it, and the latter two. These conveyances have coverings or hoods, so that ladies can go about in them quite well at night or in wet weather, and the *jampannies* are so expert at carrying them, that there is hardly any ground so rough or bad that they will not get safely over it.

The climate in the hills is, as a rule, all that can be desired. The first two months of the summer season are perfectly bright and fine every day, and now and then the heat is a little oppressive, perhaps, but never anything to speak of, and the nights are always cool. This is the great time for picnics, and, indeed, gaiety of all sorts; for people think, I suppose, that it is best to get what amusement they can before the rains set in. When these come on, life in the hills is not so pleasant, for it rains almost every day, and the stations are constantly enveloped in clouds, everything is reeking with wet and damp, and it is no joke having to ride five or six miles on a pony through a pouring rain to dine out, as may easily happen to you in Simla. It rains, too, in India in a manner of which people who live in England have but little idea. I have seen fifteen inches fall in the twenty-four hours, and when the landslip at Naini Tal took place, there were forty-two inches of rain in thirty-six hours, or more than the rainfall of the whole year in England.

About the middle of September or so, fine weather sets in, and from then till December is, to my mind, the most perfect time in the hills all the year round. The trees on every side are covered with ferns and creepers, the product of three months' rain, and these with the autumn tints on them form a lovely picture. The air is bright and clear with the crispness of approaching winter in it, and now is the time for those who care about splendid views. I know of no finer panorama than that which can be seen from the top of Cheena, the highest point in Naini Tal, on almost any morning soon after the cessation of the rains. Looking over one shoulder, you see the Himalayas stretching away before you for miles and miles to the east and west in an unbroken snow-clad line, with the lower hills and green valleys between yourself and them. Though really many miles distant, they seem, owing to the clearness of the atmosphere, quite close, and the more so as it is easy, if there is any wind blowing, to see the snow being carried away off the peaks in little white clouds. You turn and look over the other shoulder, and there, lying below you, stretch out the plains to Bareilly and Moradabad, a distance of seventy miles, with forest patches of the Terai dotted about, and different streams shining in their course from the hills through the plains. The distance you can see is really only limited by the power of your vision, and, as I have said, I have never seen anything more beautiful or wonderful than the scene which may be surveyed from Cheena. No less beautiful is it to go up there about sunset and watch the rays of the setting sun casting many-coloured tints on the snow-clad peaks, and shining on the rivers as it descends to the horizon.

For scenery, I doubt if there are many countries which can beat the Himalayas; and as far as climate is concerned, if a man is fortunate enough to be one of those officials who spend their cold weather in the plains and their hot weather in the hills, he has very little to complain of.

If children are sent or taken to the hills every hot weather, they may very well remain in India either till it is time for the boys to go to school, or until the girls are eleven or twelve years old, but they should not be kept in the plains during the hot weather after five or six years of age.

Altogether there can be no question that India is a very wonderful country, and decidedly the place for a poor man. For instance, no military officer can serve in England who has not private means; but if a man can manage to get on till he has passed from the English into the Indian service, he will find that he can live quite well on his pay. If he is a hard-working man, his chances of remunerative employment are always good, and he is far more likely to see active service in India than in any other part of Her Majesty's dominions.

The Indian Civil Service is a fine profession for those who can get into it; but in these days of competition to succeed in doing so requires such an amount of cramming, that a boy when he has distanced others is pretty well worked out, and the first thing he needs is complete rest for some time.

And now I have done. My object has been to give a brief account of life in India, and I trust that what I have written may be of service to some of those who go out there, either profes-

8

sionally or merely as travellers to see the country; and not without interest to those who know nothing of India and are not likely to visit it.